Fixing America:

A Common Man's View

Tim C. Smith

Fixing America: A Common Man's View

Copyright © 2009 by Tim C. Smith

All rights reserved. No part of this book may be reproduced or transmitted in any form or by any means without written permission of the author.

ISBN 1449537618

Dedication

To my wife, Sherrie, who has been an inspiration to me since the day we married.

To my children, Heath, Whitney, Ashley, and Brett, who have made my life both fun and interesting.

To my mother, Faye Smith, who fought Lou Gehrig's Disease to the end.

To my sisters, Tammy and Sherry, who have always been there for me. And to the rest of my family who are always there to support me through the tough times.

To Calvin Louie, the truest friend anyone could ever have.

And to Spanky and Molly, the two dogs who love me no matter what.

Foreword

Even though we live in a country that has more freedoms than any other in the world, we are slowly giving up those freedoms for hollow promises from a government that has become corrupt and concerned only with itself.

As this book is written, we currently have a deficit of over nine trillion dollars and it continues to grow. Spending is out of control and it seems like our elected officials are not listening to us or working in our best interest. While our elected officials are partly at fault, we Americans have to take a lot of the blame. We continue to elect the same people over and over rather than make the necessary changes to correct the situation.

While I write this book, the democrats in Congress want to pass legislation to give more food stamps and aid to people who don't work in order to stimulate the economy. This brings up two questions that need to be answered. First, is how in the world is this going to stimulate the economy? Second, how can our government justify doing this when they already have over a nine trillion dollar deficit?

The republicans in Congress are just as bad. Both groups want to spend more money that America does not have, they just differ on what they want to spend it on. The sad part to me is that we sit back and take it. I will never understand why Americans look to the government to save them when the government can't even save itself.

My goal in writing this book is to spell out some of the major issues that we have in this country and then provide common sense solutions. I don't know about everyone else, but I'm tired of hearing these two parties hammer away at the same problems, while giving no solutions to them.

One of the things that really bothers me is how the government deals with a problem when they don't get their way. Illegal immigration is a perfect example of this. When the American people spoke out against a bill that would have allowed amnesty, Congress backed off the passage of the bill to save their jobs. The problem is that they have done nothing since then to stem the flow of illegal immigrants that are coming across our border. Since they didn't get their way, they have simply chosen to not act at all, which allows illegal immigration to continue.

Congress gets away with this because we the people have let the issue drop. They didn't pass the amnesty bill so we think we have won a victory and just go back to business as usual. This allows the issue to die down and in a year or two Congress will be able to bring it back up and push the bill through before we even realize what has happened.

You may think this sounds radical, but we should be in the streets protesting everyday over Congresses failure to act. We should be writing letters and making phone calls to our representatives until they have no choice but to act.

My hope for this book is that it angers the people who read it to the point that they stand up and let their voices be heard. All I want to do is what any common person would do, which is to examine the problems we have and then apply common sense to solve them. Our politicians want you to think that there are no easy answers to many of our problems, but that is simply not the truth.

Neither of the two political parties that we currently have in power is looking out for us. If you think they are concerned about anyone but themselves you are sadly mistaken. I hope that you will read this book, take a good long look at what is going on around you, and then look in the mirror and ask yourself one question. Do I really want to rely on the government to take care of me or do I want to be free to take care of myself?

Table of Contents

A Common Man 1

Illegal Immigration 8

Congressional Term Limits 17

Changing Our Legal System 23

Economy 30

Tax System 40

Foreign Policy 46

Conclusion 54

About the Author 67

Chapter 1

A Common Man

Let me start this book by giving you a little history about myself. I was born and raised in a little town in North Carolina. It was a town that was built out of necessity. A man by the name of Charles Cannon built a textile mill there and he needed workers for that mill. He brought workers in and built houses, schools and stores which turned the area into a close knit community.

When I was growing up, most of my friends' parents worked in the mill. My mother and father both worked there for awhile, but my Dad hated working inside, so he learned to build houses. My mother continued to work in textile mills until she retired. My Dad only had an eighth grade education, but after he learned how to build houses, he went to the local bank and talked them into loaning him the money so that he could start building houses on his own rather than working for someone else. He worked hard and became financially successful until the late seventies and early eighties. He invested in land to start building subdivisions, but then the recession of the late seventies hit and he lost everything. He had a heart attack during this time and ended up on disability for the rest of his life.

From age nine to about fourteen I worked for him during the summer. I hauled brick and mixed mortar for the brick crew and sometimes he loaned me out to the roofer. I didn't mind the brick work, but helping the roofer was tough. My Dad paid me a dollar an hour and I worked about fifty hours a week. I thought I was rich and I was so tired at the end of each day that it helped keep me out of trouble. After we lost everything, I mowed yards and worked with horses to make money. A man that lived a few miles from us bought wild horses and I would break them and train them. One of my fondest memories is the day I got on one horse that had never been ridden. She reared and bucked a few times and then began to back up. She was backing toward the electric fence that we used to pasture them. My Dad realized what was happening and he ran to unplug the fence, but he was too late. The fence only put off six volts of electricity, but it was more than enough to put me and the horse in forward motion. I held on for dear life and she finally stopped running after a couple of miles. Needless to say, I couldn't get her to back up after that.

When I turned sixteen, I went to work for Kentucky Fried Chicken. At eighteen I graduated high school, got married shortly there after and had a baby before I was nineteen. I was way too young to get married much less have a child. After a year of installing carpet, I realized that I needed a college education, so I worked different jobs until I received an Associate degree in Criminal Justice. I then worked at a juvenile training school for three years as I worked on my Bachelors. The funny thing is the best paying job I had during this time was with United Parcel Service. They liked to hire college kids for the docks because driver positions didn't come open very often and most college kids didn't plan to stay around after they graduated in order to try and move up to a driving position. I thought I was going to die my first day unloading tractor trailers. Many people quit the first day because the work was so fast paced and hard. I ended up staying there for six years after I graduated college because jobs in the field of social work weren't very plentiful and didn't pay as well.

 During this time period I was divorced with two children to raise. My mother lived next door and stayed with the kids at night because I had to be at work at four in the morning until about eight thirty. It was part time but it still paid well. I started my own little construction business during the day. I would stop working around two and pick my oldest up from school and then get my youngest from daycare.

I did this for six years until I met and married my current wife. We moved to Georgia and I tried to start a construction business here, but it was so cut throat that I ended up going to work for the Department of Family and Children Services for three years. After three years of low pay and long hours, I received the opportunity to work in the field of insurance sales and I have been there ever since.

I give this history to make people understand that I have been through hard times just like everyone else. My first wife and I were on the WIC program for milk, but I worked my way off of that as soon as I could. I know people need help at times, but I don't think we should take advantage of it or allow ourselves to become dependent on government hand outs.

No matter what life threw at me, I knew that everything would work out and so I never gave up. I think this was because of the work ethic that my parents instilled in me. Both my parents taught me to not give up and work hard and I would be able to achieve anything that I wanted too.

My Mom worked harder than anybody I've ever known and she never relied on the government to help her through the hard times.

Just like me, she feels that our government is way too free in giving away taxpayer money, but part of that is our fault. We have allowed ourselves to fall into the trap of wanting more than we need or can afford. My wife and I were able to work hard and get our fifteen year mortgage paid off in about eight years. Our cars were paid for and we could have started putting money away and made investments to secure our future. Instead, we had friends that had just moved into a new neighborhood just a few miles from where we were living. The houses were nicer and the neighborhood had sidewalks and nicer amenities. After some discussion, we decided to buy the cheapest house in the neighborhood.

I told myself that it would be a good investment, which in reality it is, but it caused us to have to go in debt for the difference of what we made from the old house and the cost of the new one. Since it was a nicer neighborhood, of course we had to buy nicer cars and before I knew it, we were in debt again. We were fortunate not to have to finance that much on the house, so our debt is pretty low, but when I talk to a lot of the people in the neighborhood, it amazes me how deep in debt they are. Many are making six figure salaries, but it takes everything they make just to pay the bills. If they should lose their job due to a slowing economy, they have nothing set aside in order to keep paying the bills until they find something else. The amount of stress and pressure they have put on themselves is amazing to me. The really sad part is that our neighborhood is not even that expensive in comparison to the ones around it.

Our government does the same thing and we allow it to happen. The difference is that we pay for our own debt and for the debt that the politicians put us in, while they get rich with very little consequence for their action.

As I am writing this book, we have a presidential election coming up in a couple of months. When I talk to people, many of them have the same feeling that I do. We feel like we are voting for the lesser of two evils. Neither candidate has ever shown a desire to do the will of the people in their Congressional career, why should we think they would be any different as President?

While I do have a helpless feeling in the pit of my stomach, I know from history that one person can influence hundreds that can grow into thousands and then millions. Once an idea obtains the momentum of the people, it is almost impossible to stop and that is when change occurs.

I have no political experience, but I do feel like I have a lot of common sense and life experience, just like the majority of Americans do. We're not as dumb as the politicians seem to think.

It's time that we band together and use the power that we have been given to get change implemented. In the following chapters, I've outlined a plan that this common man thinks will work. Our system is broken and we must try something different in order to fix it.

Chapter 2

Illegal Immigration

Illegal immigration is one of the biggest problems that we face in America. I will be the first to admit that America has always been known as the great melting pot. Our society is made up of immigrants from all over the world. The only Native Americans are the American Indians. Don't get me wrong, I don't have a problem with people wanting to immigrate to America. When you look at how good we've had it for so long, it's easy to understand why people would want to live here.

When America was first established, there was a big need for immigration. The country was young and the best way to populate it was through immigration. In fact it was necessary to build the population in order to secure the country. The more people we had the bigger we could build our army and the better we could protect our country.

To me, it's ironic that one of the things that helped build our country is now one of the biggest threats we have. Our nation has grown to a point where we have to rethink both legal and illegal immigration. While we still have a need for immigration, we can now choose who we allow in and who we turn away.

With our current immigration policy, it allows too many criminal elements to enter our society and create a whole new set of problems for its citizens. It seems that our elected officials don't understand the problems with illegal immigration. The Democratic Party even wants to give illegal immigrants the right to vote. They want to do this because they feel that illegals will vote for them and help them to retain their power. It's amazing to me that our politicians just don't take time to really look at the situation and the problems that are occurring because they continue to ignore the wishes of the American people.

The first problem is the crimes committed by illegal immigrants. Now, I know that many of these people are hard workers and are just looking for a better way of life. The problem is that there are quite a few that come here and commit horrible acts of criminal violence. If you don't believe me, just check your local paper's police blotter or watch the news. What makes it worse is that many times these criminals are hard to catch because they are illegal and it is hard to identify them because there is no record of their existence in our society. If the police do catch them, then we the taxpayers have to pay to support them while they do their time in our jails.

The second problem is the drain they put on our health care system. Most of them are paid low wages and can't afford health insurance. What they have learned is they can go into any public hospital and get treated for anything from the common cold to cancer and not have to pay a dime. Hospitals in border towns are especially hard hit. Many are on the verge of going bankrupt and in turn they have to pass the cost for the illegal's on to the consumers and insurance companies that can pay. That in turn drives up the cost of health care that the legal citizens of this country have to pay.

The third problem is that they undercut businesses owned by American citizens. Most of these immigrants quickly realize that they can start their own construction type services and perform them cheaper, because they do not carry general liability or workers comp, like American citizens are required to do. Trust me, when you have a problem arise on a job that can cause a loss of money or injury to someone, you will wish you had hired a company that had insurance. In some ways, they are much better at handling finances than we are. Five or six of them will rent one house and then share the expenses. By doing this, they are able to lower their prices even more so that normal business can't compete. I hear from contractors all the time that tell me about the work they have lost because someone who is here illegally undercut them on price. Most of the time, the illegal's don't even have the experience to know how to do a job.

We found out too late that the contractor who built our first house in Georgia had used mainly illegals to do the work. According to building code the two by four studs that make the walls in a house are supposed to be sixteen inches in distance from the center of one to the center of the next. Imagine my aggravation and surprise when I went to hang sheetrock in our basement and I found that the studs varied in distance. Some were fourteen inches apart and others were seventeen inches apart. They were close enough for an inspector to pass and the house was sturdy, but it cost me about twenty five percent extra in material because I had to either put in extra studs or cut and waste sheetrock. It's no fun when you go to put up a piece of sheetrock and find that the end is about two inches short of the last stud because the studs aren't evenly placed. In this case, I don't blame the illegals, I blame the contractor who hired them and didn't even try to give them the proper guidance they needed to do the job correctly. I have many other examples from that same house, but I think you get the picture.

The final problem that I will discuss is the jobs they take. I know that most people would say that the illegal immigrants fill jobs that Americans won't do. While this may be true, the main reason for this is because Americans have been conditioned by our politicians to believe they need to rely on the government to meet their needs. In reality, all it does is keep people from working to better themselves and achieve the American dream.

While there are other problems that are caused by illegal immigration, I think you get the basic idea. The good news is there are pretty simple solutions to all the problems caused by illegal immigration. All of the solutions are based on common sense.

I know there are a lot of people out there that will think I'm crazy, but the first thing I think we need to do is put up at least a fence, preferably a wall. I'm not sure why so many people seem to think this is a radical idea. To me, it only makes sense. A wall will enable the U.S. to control the borders with a minimum amount of man power. It would be extremely expensive and impractical to try and hire enough border patrol agents to stem the flow of illegal immigrants coming into this country. While a wall would be expensive on the front end, the amount of man power needed to patrol the wall would be a quarter of what is needed to adequately patrol the border without a wall.

The purpose of the wall wouldn't be to stop immigration, just illegal immigration. We have laws for a reason and we must enforce them for the betterment of society. So, even though many illegals may be coming to America looking for a better life, we cannot reward them for breaking the law. With a wall we could allow legal immigrants a chance at a better life, without allowing the criminal element to penetrate our borders so easily.

Would this stop illegal immigration all together? Of course not, because there is no perfect solution. It would, however, greatly reduce the amount of illegal immigrants who are able to get through and it would make it very hard for them to smuggle drugs across the border.

Once we have stopped the influx of illegal's coming across the border, the next thing to do would be to round up the illegal immigrants currently living in the U.S. While this may seem harsh to some people it's something that must be done. No matter how nice they may be or how good their intentions are, they are still in violation of our laws. We also need to change the current laws that allow citizenship to the children of illegal's just for being born here. I'm sorry, but no other country allows citizenship based purely on birth. If you go to China and have a baby while you're there, I can assure you the Chinese government won't make that child a citizen just because they were born there.

There is a solution for those who have been here and have been contributing to society in a positive way. If they are willing to serve in the U.S. military for a minimum of five years, then I would say they have earned their citizenship. We expect our current citizens to put their lives on the line, so anyone that wants to earn their citizenship should be willing to do the same.

Putting up the wall and dealing with the problem of the illegals that are already here would also help to stop the drain on our hospitals and health care facilities, but we would also need to pass legislation to deal with this. I think hospitals should help our citizens and legal immigrants who don't have insurance, but they can't do it for free. Legislation needs to be passed that would require the hospitals to treat people who are uninsured, but then enable them to garnish a small percent of their wages until the bill is paid. If they aren't employed then let them do work around the hospital until the debt is paid. Hospitals have expenses they have to pay and it's only fair that we all pay our part if we use their services.

Like I said before, a few illegals may still get past the wall. For that reason we need to implement laws that will make immigrants less likely to want to come here illegally. We need to place heavy fines on businesses that hire illegals and then use our current resources to enforce these fines. If a business continues to violate the law despite the fines, then we need to add jail time for repeat offenders. This would make it almost impossible for illegals to obtain jobs here and they would be less likely to try and come here illegally.

The final argument I hear is that immigrants fill jobs that most Americans won't. While I will be the first to admit this is true to a degree, there is a simple solution to this. I will deal with this more in a later chapter on economics, but for now suffice it to say, our society is teaching its citizens to be dependent on government welfare. If we end welfare as we know it and just provide for child care so that the current recipients would be forced to work, we would have the people we need to fill the jobs that are out there and hopefully it would cause them to have higher self esteem and a better standard of living.

Our politicians want to make everything harder than it is. Illegal immigration is a problem that can be solved like most other problems. All we have to do is use a little thing called common sense. I know that our wonderful politicians will say that it's just not that simple. If they were honest, they would admit that some things are that simple. It's time we raise our voices and let them know we want them to deal with illegal immigration and stop putting it on a back burner until it is convenient for them.

Chapter 3

Congressional Term Limits

It has always astounded me that the President can only serve two terms of four years, but a congressman can stay in office until he dies if he chooses. Now, don't get me wrong. I don't want to set the Presidency up for someone to stay in the position for life. What I am proposing is that we set term limits on Congress.

The best example of the need for term limits is Senator Strom Thurmond of South Carolina. Senator Thurmond was in office for 48 years. He retired from the senate at age one hundred and died about 6 months after he retired. The last ten years that he was in office, he was too sick to attend congressional meetings and perform his duties. Now, I know that most people gain wisdom as they grow older by learning from the mistakes of their youth, but there is a point when a person reaches an age where they really need to turn the reins over to the next generation.

As I write this book, long term Senator Edward Kennedy has been diagnosed with cancer. Senator Kennedy has to undergo chemo-therapy and radiation and even then his survival is not certain. It's going to be very hard for him to fulfill his duties as a Senator, so you would think that he would step down and let the people choose someone to replace him. If you think that, you would be wrong. Senator Kennedy wants to put his wife in Congress to fill in for him until he can return to his duties or until the people vote him and his wife out. My question would be where does Senator Kennedy get the right to decide who takes his place? Of course you can't totally blame Senator Kennedy for this. The people of Massachusetts have to take some responsibility for not being outraged and shooting down his effort to give his office to his wife.

    One of the other problems that we face with these lifetime congress people is they forget who sent them there and why. I think that many of these elected officials have good intentions when they first make it to Washington, but the longer they are there, the more they lose touch with the people that put them there. They sell out to special interest groups in order to get reelected term after term. Now, why would they be concerned with what the average person thinks when it's the special interest groups that are getting them elected? Term limits might not totally eliminate this problem, but it would definitely improve the situation. We would also need to find a way to limit the money that these special interest groups donate to different candidates.

I've watched presidential debates many times and one of the things that drives me crazy is when they talk about inexperience. While I think that a presidential candidate needs life experience, sometimes I think they may have way too much political experience. The majority of our politicians today seem to try and solve the same problems over and over with the same worn out ineffective solutions. When a new Congressman comes to Capital Hill, they usually have all kinds of new ideas and they are excited to think that they may have a chance to truly improve our country. What usually happens is the senior members of Congress quickly bring them in line to the old way of thinking.

We the people have to step up and say enough is enough. It amazes me that we continue to vote the same people into office term after term. When you look into the records of these life time Congressional members, you'll find they have accomplished very little and most of what they have accomplished is for the special interest groups. We have a new weapon in our arsenal to aid us in determining if a Congressman is doing their job. It's called the Internet. We can use it to look up the voting records of each member of

Congress. Before you try to tell others how great a particular Congressperson is, you should look up their record. You might be amazed at how little they have actually accomplished. You'll find that many of them haven't even been there to vote for many of the more important issues on the table. They do this so that they can avoid making a decision that may be unpopular and that may come back to bite them when they run for reelection or if they make a run for the presidency.

Many people will say that their political party and political candidates are looking out for them. The hard truth is, whether you're a Republican or Democrat, these people are only out for one thing, and that's power. Term limits and our current tax codes give them that power. Until enough people have gotten tired of these career politicians, the only changes that will occur in Washington won't be to the benefit of the American people.

One of the things that we need in setting term limits is to fine tune the political process. These candidates raise and spend millions in their election runs. Most of the money comes from special interest groups that have the politicians in their back pocket. This makes it very hard for a third party to be able to rise up and give the American people more choices.

Don't get me wrong, I don't think that running for public office should place a hardship on candidates. I just think that limiting the amount of money a candidate can raise would even the playing field for all candidates and give the people a sense of how a candidate handles their money. If they're able to stay in the campaign on a budget and get their names out to the people, that shows they may have the ability to handle the money of the people.

The same tool I mentioned before is available for all the candidates to use and at a very cheap price. Every citizen in the U.S. has access to the Internet, if not at home, then through the public library. Each candidate should be able to set up a web site letting people know what they plan to do and what they stand for. There would be no need for the high dollar television ads and radio commercials. If a citizen is too lazy to take the time to look up the candidates on line, then they shouldn't be voting. We the people have to take some responsibility for reigning in our government and the only way to do it is by being well informed voters.

Every one of us should be contacting our Congress person weekly and telling them we want term limits set. If they don't listen, then we need to vote out the incumbent every time an election comes around until they understand that we no longer want lifers in the Congress. It amazes me to hear people complain over and over about Congress and the President, yet they continue to vote in the same people every time an election year rolls around. It's time for American citizens to impose their will on the officials we elect. If we don't, then we will be to blame for the demise of America as we know it. The best way to kill democracy is for the masses to fail to act in an informed way.

Chapter 4

Changing Our Legal System

I've been selling insurance for about eight years now. Whenever I go to renew a policy I usually hear the same thing from clients. "These insurance companies are ripping me off. These premiums are outrageous." I usually just listen to them and let them vent. When they finish complaining, I look them in the eye and tell them that I agree that the premiums are too high, but then I tell them that it's not the insurance company's fault that the premiums continue to climb. When they look at me like they think I'm stupid, I smile at them and inform them they can blame our legal system and the wonderful lawyers in Congress.

One of my favorite examples of this is the lady who sued McDonalds because she spilled coffee in her lap and it burned her. She sued McDonalds claiming that the coffee was too hot and that's why she was burned. It evidently had nothing to do with her being a klutz. The funny thing is, if the coffee had been cold, she would have taken it back inside and complained because it wasn't hot.

Another great example was an insurance client that had a crime committed against him and was then sued by the criminal's family. The client, who was in his office one day a little after five, had already locked the door for the business and was finishing some paper work before heading home. As he sat there doing his job, a man started beating on the door. The client went to the door and quickly realized that the man was on some type of drugs, so he decided not to open the door. The man began to hit the glass on the door with a rock trying to get it to break. The client ran back to his desk and called 911. The client had the police on the phone, when he heard the glass begin to break. The client was smart enough to have a permit to carry a gun, so he had one at work with him. He yelled for the criminal to stop trying to break in or he would shoot. The criminal finished breaking the glass and started toward the client. The criminal was much bigger than the client, so after one last warning, the client shot the criminal several times until the criminal finally fell to his knees and quit coming toward the client. The police arrived, took the man to a local hospital where he recovered and was quickly whisked away to jail. The client was found to have acted in self defense and the criminal case was done. What happened next in civil court was the shocking part. The criminal's wife sued the client for loss of consortion. The client and the insurance company went to court and a jury awarded her a million dollars even though her husband was in the process of committing a felony. These kind of suits need to be stopped and a loser pay system put in place.

Now I know this is just one example, but this is truly an every day occurrence. What the average person doesn't know, but all lawyers do, is that insurance companies will usually settle out of court because it is cheaper than trying to fight in court. If the insurance company has to go to court it will cost them twenty thousand dollars in attorney fees and court costs just for the first hearing. The lawyers know this and so they will negotiate with insurance companies for settlements of ten to fifteen thousand dollars.

The majority of settlements I have observed with our court system are on the civil side. I know that there are a lot of people out there that think the big bad insurance companies and the corporations they represent won't be hurt if they have to pay out money on bogus claims. The truth is that it doesn't really affect the insurance companies. It's the average people like you and me that pay for these outrageous claims. Insurance companies have to make money to stay in business, so when they pay out too much, they simply raise the price of their product. It's the same thing with corporations.

When they have to pay out money on ridiculous lawsuits, then they have to increase prices or lay off workers.

Congress is full of lawyers, so who do you think they will favor when they create or fail to create new laws? That's right, it's all about them. They design it so that their profession can live the high life at our expense. Mostly what they do is fail to act in creating laws that would help to prevent frivolous lawsuits.

There was a time when lawyers weren't allowed to advertise on television. Congress changed the laws dealing with this so that lawyers could advertise, which I think was the right thing to do. The problem is that they didn't put certain controls on the situation.

For instance, I had a friend who was in an automobile accident that wasn't his fault. Thankfully he received only a few minor bruises and his car had minor damage. When he awoke the morning after the accident, he was a little sore so he decided to take the day off from work. He told me later that his phone rang about twice an hour all day long. He answered the first four or five times, but soon stopped answering at all. The reason he stopped answering was because the calls were coming from attorneys. They had somehow found out about his wreck and they wanted to help him sue for all that they felt he deserved for the ordeal he had just gone through. They assured him that they only got paid if they were able to get a settlement for him. None of these attorneys wanted to tell him how much of the settlement they would take, but he finally got one to admit that they usually received around forty percent. My friend politely declined their offers, went back to work the next day and the at fault driver's insurance paid for his car to be fixed. All of this was accomplished without an attorney.

The question that my friend and I both asked was how did the attorneys find out about the accident and get his information to call him? Most likely they got it from the local police department where police reports are easily accessible. My point is that there should be controls in place so that these attorneys can't get this information and then try and pressure people into filing lawsuits that aren't justified.

I'm all for someone being able to sue when they have truly been hurt by someone else's negligence, but I think anything can be carried too far.

Our legal system needs to be changed. First on the criminal side, we need to take out the televisions and workout equipment. I once worked as a prison guard and the only riot we had while I was there was over the fact that the power went out and they were unable to watch the Mike Tyson fight on HBO. This was in the eighties and I was still using rabbit ears on my television at home. I'm sorry, but if someone commits a crime, they should have only the basics of life. They need to be working out in the field growing their own food and physically hammering big rocks into small ones. If we make it tough on them when they are in prison, they're less likely to want to go back when they get out. They are also less likely to cause problems while they are in prison. It's unfair to expect a guard to be able to control prisoners that have had nothing to do all day but lift weights and think of ways to cause trouble. If they were to work all day, they would be too tired to cause problems.

    Next, we need to change the civil side to a loser pay system. The way it is now, if someone files a bogus lawsuit and they lose, it only costs them their attorney fees. If the attorneys take the case pro bono and lose it only costs them their time. With a loser pay system, the loser and their attorney would have to cover the cost of whoever they sued. This would stop these lawyers from calling accident victims and convincing them to file lawsuits.

    We also need to change the civil side so that jury trials aren't used initially. When a suit is filed, you have to go by the evidence and try to limit the involvement of personal feelings. I think this would be better accomplished by a judge making the decision based on the evidence. If the judge decides against the claimant, then they can file an appeal and a jury trial can be allowed at that level. Most lawyers won't be willing to take their bogus suit to the next level because it would cost them too much.

By changing our legal system we can achieve a couple of things. First, we can get rid of costly lawsuits that tie up our legal system and drive up insurance prices. Secondly, it will help cut government spending on prison systems, because we can let them grow their own food and hopefully cut back on the number of prisons we need since criminals will think twice about committing crimes and going to prison.

Most criminals are not concerned with the rights of their victims, so why should we be concerned with the rights of criminals. In my opinion the only right they have is to work and be fed and clothed while they are in the prison. When they decided to commit a crime, they gave up any rights they had. If we continue to make prisons more appealing to them than the life they have on the outside, our prisons are only going to continue to grow. It's time to take a stand and make a change in the way our legal system works.

Chapter 5

Economy

Even in the bad times, America has set the economic standard for the rest of the world. No other country displays the attributes of capitalism like the United States. For over two hundred years, people from all other nations have flocked to America because it is the land of opportunity.

Now, you would think that our government would be proud of this and encourage our economy, but they seem to be doing just the opposite. First, they pass laws that raise taxes for American businesses trying to use American workers. This results in big corporations outsourcing their business to other countries because services and products produced overseas are cheaper due to imports not being taxed as high as services and products made in the good old USA.

If you don't believe me just look at the products you buy. You will find that most products are made in China or Korea. Having a problem with your cell phone or computer? Just call the help desk number and you will find yourself talking to someone in India. Why would our elected officials not only allow this to occur, but seem to encourage it? The answer is simple; money and power. If you do your homework and check into it, you will find that most of them have investments in overseas companies and they receive special treatment from foreign countries in return for driving American jobs overseas. They are looking out for their best interest and not putting America first.

    Politicians achieve their goals through media manipulation and the mis-education of the American people. They have used the media to guide us away from the truth and the public education system to train us to blindly follow those in charge. It's amazing to me that we will accept as truth pretty much anything the media tells us without using the resources we have in this country to check out the facts. If we were to take time to check out the stories that the news media puts out, we would find that the majority are either not true or grossly exaggerated. Many times they will tell just one side of the story and not give us all the facts. Democrats blame Republicans, Republicans blame Democrats, and the news media helps to keep us confused and misinformed. The media will blame the economic woes on the war in Iraq, the housing crisis, corporate greed and so forth. Very few media outlets will tell you where the real problem lies.

Fixing America

The real problem lies with too much government control. Our school systems are an excellent example of government control. Government schools teach our kids that everything should be shared equally in society. If someone can't afford to buy school supplies, then those who can should provide enough for everyone. Don't get me wrong, I don't mind helping someone who is trying to help themselves, but I refuse to help people who think our society owes them something and they shouldn't have to work hard to improve their status in life.

I worked for a small business once that was bought out by a big corporation. The owners of the small business came along with the buy out and some of the employees found out that they were receiving huge annual bonuses for staying and getting the employees to stay. These employees griped and complained that they didn't think the old owners deserved these bonuses. When they griped to me, my answer was simple. My feeling was, these owners had taken the chance of starting a small business and had built it into a very lucrative deal that had created over one hundred jobs for the communities where they were located. They took the chance so they deserved whatever they received. You should be rewarded based on the risk you take and the work you put in. Our education system promotes just the opposite behavior. With the help of Congress and special interest groups, the education system basically promotes socialism, which in turn promotes government control.

What I want people to do is ask themselves a simple question. When the government gets overly involved in anything does it seem to help or hurt? When you ask yourself this question, I want you to think about our social security system, Medicare, and our current tax system. Social Security and Medicare will be bankrupted in the next twenty years if something isn't done. Do you know of anyone who really understands our tax system? Just try and read any part of our current tax code and see how much of it you can understand.

As I write this book, our President and Congress have approved a tax rebate to try and stimulate our economy. Families can get back as much as twelve hundred dollars to spend anyway they choose. The hope is that people will spend the money to purchase products and services and thus stimulate the economy. This is like trying to put a band-aid on a severed limb. It may give a temporary boost, but most people will probably use the money to pay off debt and the economy won't be any better.

The sad part is that there are some simple answers to our economic troubles, but it takes power away from the government. The first thing we need to do is pass the Fair Tax put forth by Georgia Republican John Linder. The current tax code is too complicated and places the majority of the tax burden on the middle class. The Fair Tax would distribute the tax burden equally, and eliminate the need for the Internal Revenue Service as it currently exists. I'm not going to get into the details of the Fair Tax here, but it would be the best economic stimulus package we could ask for. Congressman Linder and radio personality, Neil Boortz have written two books explaining the Fair Tax in great detail. I would suggest that every American citizen read these books. Implemented correctly, the Fair Tax would help us to pay off our debt and fund social security and Medicare. This would also help to eliminate our dependence on foreign governments.

    The second thing is to limit government spending. Most of us have to live on a budget and so should our government. Government would be limited to a certain amount of money each year, which would eliminate a lot of the government waste that we see today. The budget would not be unrealistic; however, if it is done correctly, all the excess waste and spending would be eliminated. If we had special circumstances, such as a war, during which the government needed extra money, then they could raise money through bond sales just like they did in World War two.

The third thing is to stop illegal immigration and open up more jobs for Americans. Now, I know that a lot of people say that Americans wouldn't do the jobs that illegals currently fill. That may be true to a degree, but I think that we can find plenty of Americans to fill these jobs when we implement the fourth change.

The fourth thing is to end welfare as we know it. I think that our current welfare system teaches people not to work and lowers their self esteem. What I propose is that the only form of welfare we give is daycare for workers with children who make less than a certain amount per year. If a person didn't go to work, then they would receive no help at all. This may seem harsh, but I think it would do wonders for people's self esteem. Instead of having to live off of a few hundred dollars a month provided to them by the government, they would be able to earn more money and become self sufficient.

People really need to take time and think about this one. Our government seems to think they are doing something great when they send people welfare checks for five or six hundred a month. All it really does, along with government housing, is lock people into a very poor standard of living. Most people don't realize that the only people making minimum wage are usually teenagers working a part time job.

In truth, the majority of the jobs start full time workers at a minimum of eight dollars an hour. Most of these jobs will go up to ten dollars an hour or more within a two year period. They may not get rich at eight dollars an hour, but let's do the math. If a person makes eight dollars an hour and works forty hours a week, that's three hundred twenty dollars a week. That would mean that the person would make twelve hundred and eighty dollars a month. If we implement the Fair Tax that person would bring home the whole amount.

Currently most welfare recipients receive a check for around five hundred a month and then housing worth another four hundred a month. That's nine hundred a month with no hope for a raise. If we put them to work and provide daycare to get them back in the work force, they will automatically make three hundred and eighty dollars more a month with the potential for raises and a higher standard of living. In return they are now contributing to the economy. It's a win-win situation.

Fifth, we need to raise taxes on imported items, making American products and services more competitive. This would bring more jobs back to the U.S. The more industry that we bring back to America, the stronger our economy becomes. Currently we pay China, South Korea, and several other countries billions of dollars a year to make up for not exporting as much to them as they do to us. This doesn't make sense to me. Why should we pay them one single dime? Instead we should make it cost as much for them to do business in the U.S. as it cost for American based companies to do business here. What most people don't realize is that a lot of the products and services they receive from other countries are financed with U.S money from corporations and politicians here. It's cheaper for them do it this way, than for them to actually have these products made in America. Our politicians are getting rich with no concern for how it affects our country and we just keep letting them get away with it.

Finally, as stated in the previous chapter, we need a full overhaul of our legal system. We have too many frivolous lawsuits being filed and clogging up our legal system and it has to stop. We need to implement some sort of loser pay system and possibly do away with jury trials in certain civil suit situations.

I know a lot of people would disagree with doing away with the jury trial in some civil suits, but let's look at the problem with the jury trial in civil suits. I think we can all agree that most people on a jury don't know or understand the law in civil suits. In criminal cases, juries are told the offense that was committed and then shown the evidence to allow them to make an informed decision. Empathy can play a role in a criminal case, but juries don't usually empathize with criminals. In civil cases the lawyer for the plaintiff focuses on getting the jury to empathize with their client. Many of the people on a civil jury are able to put themselves in the place of the plaintiff, which means they aren't able to keep emotion out of the process. The result is frivolous lawsuits being paid out of empathy rather than making a decision based on the facts.

 A loser pay system would help keep lawyers from calling injured people and talking them into filing frivolous lawsuits. As this book is written, a lawsuit has just been filed that that illustrates what I've been saying. A seventeen year old was killed at a local theme park, when he jumped over two fence barriers on a ride and ignored all warning signs. His parents have now filed a suit against the theme park. While I feel sympathy for the parents, the question I have is why did he jump the fences and where were his parents? A seventeen year old should know better than to ignore the safety features that the park put in place, and if he didn't know any better, then his parents should have been there to stop him. My guess is that some lawyer contacted the family not long after it happened and told them that while he couldn't replace their son, he could help ease their pain by filing a suit against the park and making them rich. I'm sorry, but I don't see that the theme park has any responsibility in what happened. They did their due diligence to keep people safe, but they can't control people who don't follow the rules. If a loser pay system was in place, these lawyers wouldn't be so quick to talk people into filing suit. The other problem in this case is that it will probably go before a jury and out of sympathy they will award the parents some type of settlement. Seventy percent of that settlement or better will most likely go to the lawyer. This doesn't include all the court costs and the time that is wasted by our courts. Something has got to change.

    There are many other problems that we need to work on, but if we deal with these six major ones, we will make our economy the strongest on this globe. It won't happen overnight, but it will happen if we use the power of our vote and raise our voices high.

Chapter 6

Tax System

During the civil war our government began an income tax in order to have the money to fight to hold our nation together. The tax was only supposed to last until the war was over. As you now know, it has lasted much longer than it was suppose too. In all honesty, it has not only survived, but it has grown bigger than anyone could've ever have imagined.

When I was a kid, I was taught to give a tenth of whatever I earned to my church for the service of God. Somehow it just doesn't seem right that I now have to pay thirty-five percent of what I make to the government when God only asks for ten percent. The sad part is that it is only going to get worse unless we do something to change it.

April fifteenth has become a day of fear and confusion. The way it is suppose to work is that we pay a percentage of tax based on how much we make and the number of dependents we have. Sounds pretty simple, right? Well if it is so simple, why is it that I claim two dependents every year, when I really have four, and yet I still owe taxes at the end of the year? According to our tax laws, the company I work for should be withholding a certain amount of money for taxes based on what I make and the dependents I claim. This means if I claim two dependents when I really have four, then I should be getting a tax refund every year. Somehow I always end up owing money and that just doesn't make sense to me.

Our current tax system puts the majority of the tax burden on the middle class. Most politicians want you to believe if they are elected, they will increase taxes on the wealthy and relieve the burden on the middle class. There are a couple of problems with this. First, any family making over sixty thousand a year is considered to be wealthy. Second, they're not telling you that they get most of their money from the big corporations and special interest groups, and in return they give these groups huge tax breaks.

Now, don't get me wrong, I don't think we should place huge tax burdens on corporations. You see, the more tax breaks they can get in the U.S., the more likely they are to keep their corporate operations here and the more jobs it will create. When a corporation is burdened with heavy taxes, they simply move their operations to other countries that don't tax them as much and then ship their products back to America. Since imported goods are taxed at a low rate it is much cheaper for them to do it this way.

As I write this book, one of the presidential candidates is pushing his tax plan saying that he will increase taxes on the rich and give a tax break to the middle class and the poor. The problem is that he will be raising taxes on anyone making over two hundred thousand a year. This means that small business owners will be heavily penalized because most of them fall into this category. While they may make over two hundred thousand a year, most of that money goes back into their business. What do you think is going to happen when their tax burden is increased? They're going to have to lay off workers in order to offset this additional expense. When people get laid off our economy only gets worse. That does not sound like a good tax plan to me.

Texas is one of the fastest growing and financially secure states in the U.S. There are two reasons for this. First, they don't have state income taxes which help to draw in new business. There are several states that don't have income tax; however, the second reason is what sets Texas apart. Texas is constantly reducing their government spending. They make the tough choices that enable them to use the sales tax system to support the state's needs. They work hard to keep down government waste and as a result their economic status is extremely strong, while the federal government gets weaker by the day because it continues to increase its debt. If the system works for the state of Texas, then it should definitely work for the feds.

I am a strong supporter of a system called the Fair Tax. I realize that our government has to have money to function, but they just don't need as much as they are taking. The Fair Tax, which was introduced by Georgia Congressman John Linder, would bring the current burdensome income tax to an end and replace it with a flat sales tax. Many politicians are against this because it would take away a lot of their power.

Congress derives most of its power from special interest groups who donate to their election bids. These special interest groups usually represent big business and foreign investments. In return for the funding they give, they expect the elected officials to pass laws and tax cuts for them. Since the poor in our country pay very little in taxes, that leaves most of the tax burden on the good old middle class.

The Fair Tax, correctly implemented, would make everyone pay the same tax on goods they buy. It would help the poor in our society because taxes paid on necessities, such as groceries, would be refunded to all citizens at the end of each month. In essence, the people who are considered to be poor in this country would not pay any taxes unless they bought items unnecessary for their survival. We would still need to cut government spending and government waste, but we need to do that no matter what tax system we have.

One argument that I have heard against the Fair Tax is that it would put a lot of people out of work because there would be no need for the IRS. The truth is that most of these people would still be needed in order to make sure the monthly checks are paid back to the people for the taxes on the necessities they buy.

It has been shown in Texas that this concept works, but unfortunately the general public has not taken notice. Many economists would agree that implementation of the Fair Tax, in addition to a decrease in government spending, could fund social security, Medicare and pay off the national debt in as little as eight to ten years. This is something our current tax system can't do. Now that's an economic stimulus package that we should all want.

If we as Americans don't soon stand up and demand this type of tax reform, our economy will continue to grow weaker as other countries grow stronger from our decline. Congress needs to be forced into passing a new tax system that is fair and solves our current economic woes. Once the laws are passed, they need to be made permanent.

It would be easy for the American people to force this issue and get the necessary changes made to make our country great again. Voting is the most powerful tool that we have and we need to use it to force out incumbents at every election, who won't implement the will of the people. If we don't use our power to change the system, then don't be surprised if we lose the power we have in the future.

Chapter 7

Foreign Policy

I have to start this chapter by letting people know that I'm not one of these people that believe that America should withdraw from the world scene and just take care of it's self. Whether we want to believe it or not, there are groups of people in this would that hate us and would love to destroy the American way of life. It is my firm belief that we can either fight these people in the places where they hide or we can wait and allow them to attack us here. For those of you who say just leave them alone and they will leave us alone, I would have to wonder where you were during the two different attacks on the World Trade Center or the attack on the USS Cole. We can't just stick our heads in the sand and hope that they go away. It just isn't going to happen. I know that it is hard for some of us here in America to comprehend, but the only thing that will stop some of these groups is the use of force.

Having said that, I also don't believe that we should be going to other countries and trying to force our way of life on them. When we go into another country to fight terrorism, I don't think we should always foot the bill for rebuilding. Iraq is an excellent example of what I am talking about. If you haven't realized it yet, Saddam Hussein was a terrorist. If we had not gone after him, sooner or later he would have supported attacks on us. I have no problem with the fact that we went after him, but I do have a real problem with us footing the bill to rebuild Iraq. Iraq is a country rich with oil, yet we are spending billions of dollars a week trying to secure and rebuild them. My question is why can't we use the profits from the sale of their oil to rebuild them and to pay for our military to protect them until they are able to protect themselves? I can assure you that if Russia, China or a lot of other countries were helping Iraq, instead of us, they would have no problem using the oil to support the rebuilding effort. Being in Iraq shouldn't be costing the USA a single dime.

 The main problem the U.S. has is that we play way too nice. We're always trying to appease the rest of the world. We want to make China and South Korea happy, so we make it cheaper for them to export products to us than it is for us to manufacture the products here. This has made it virtually impossible for manufacturers here to compete and has basically driven most of them out of business. This causes our workers to be unemployed and to be looking for a different industry in which to work.

We try to appease the United Nations every time the world suffers a natural disaster. The perfect example of this is the Tsunami that hit Indonesia, Sri Lanka and India in 2004. When America announced how much it would give to help with the disaster, the United Nations complained that this was not enough and we should give more. So our wonderful government decided to appease the U.N. and consequently more than doubled its initial pledge of aid. It didn't really matter if we could afford it or not, it was what was expected of us. The funny thing is that the countries that complained the most, didn't even give half as much in aid combined as we did.

As I write this book, there is a controversy going on involving Rachel Ray of the Food Network. While filming a commercial for a company, she was wearing a black and white scarf around her neck. The Muslim population complained saying that the scarf resembled the type that Muslim men wear and it offended them for a woman to wear one like theirs. Guess what the company did? That's right; they pulled the commercial from the airwaves because they didn't want to offend anyone. Every American citizen should be so outraged by this. We should be filling the streets with demonstrations and protests. Instead, we shake our heads and ask ourselves what the world is coming to. Like it or not, when we allow these type of things to occur, we are guilty of appeasement.

While we sit back and let this type of thing happen the Muslims grow bolder in their attacks. Several cartoon artists did editorial cartoons depicting Muslims in humorous situations. The Muslim population made all kinds of threats against the artists and the papers that ran the cartoons. The papers apologized and pulled the cartoons from being run in the future. This may have been a minor thing to most people, but many of the Muslim population saw it as a victory and now they continue to wage more and more of these types of complaints against anyone who is not Muslim.

The only way to truly fix our foreign policy is to put the best interest of the United States first. Don't misunderstand me; I'm all for working with other countries to make the world a better place, just not at the cost of American jobs or lives. No other country is looking out for us, so we better start looking out for ourselves.

The first thing we need to do is increase taxes on imports so that we can level the playing field for American companies. This would enable new American companies to open and expand, creating new jobs for Americans and virtually eliminating unemployment. This in turn would strengthen our entire economy.

    Secondly, we need to stop allowing foreign countries to buy property in America. It's one thing to allow foreign countries to rent space here and compete in the U.S., but there are not many other countries that allow their land to be bought out by foreign powers. It's just not good business. As I write this, China is buying stock in our financial institutions. I was watching a news show and the interviewer was talking to the owner of a big Chinese corporation who is doing a lot of investing in the U.S. economy right now. The interviewer asked him if he allowed the Chinese government to influence his investments and his answer was not really. Then the interviewer asked him about the economic nuclear option. This is where China pulls out all of its money from the U.S. economy and basically causes our economy to collapse and pretty much devastates our country. She wanted to know if he would do something like that if his government asked him to. The interesting thing was that he didn't ever say no. What he said was that he didn't think they would ever need to do that. I don't know about you, but I don't want our country to be in this position. If we start now, we can slowly turn this around and get to a point where we would be just fine if China or any other country withdrew their finances from our economy. I think other countries investing in our economy is a good thing, I just don't want to be dependent on them.

Third, we need to stop catering to the different nations of the world and their people. While it is good to help others when you can, we need to limit the amount of aid that we give to other countries so that we quit putting our country in financial peril. This may draw complaints from other nations, but it would help us to cut our national deficit and hopefully force other countries to help out more. Right now our government seems more concerned with improving other countries while ours deteriorates rapidly. In the past we left it up to churches and other non profit organizations to help out when disaster struck and they handled it much better than our government ever has.

Finally, we need to break our dependence on other countries for things such as oil. With the technology currently available to us, there is no reason for us to have to rely on Saudi Arabia or any other country for our mobility. We currently have a deficit of over nine trillion dollars, due mostly to our dependency on oil. The U.S. bought ANWR (Arctic National

Wildlife Refuge) in Alaska because of the available oil there. Unfortunately, we began to cater to the environmentalist and now the land is just sitting there not being used. Then again, maybe it is being used. There is an indication that the Russians are starting to do diagonal drilling just outside of Alaska. Diagonal drilling allows them to tap into the oil in ANWR without the U.S. really being able to prove they are doing it. Next there is China. China is working with Cuba to drill in the ocean between Florida and Cuba, a place that we could be drilling, but once again, thanks to the appeasing of environmentalist, we're losing out.

I'm all for protecting the environment, but as I stated before, with the technology we currently have available, there is no reason we can't safely drill for oil in ANWR or off the cost of Florida. The drilling would allow us to reduce our foreign dependency on oil for the next thirty years at least, which would strengthen our economy. In those thirty years, we could come up with alternatives to gas and begin a slow switch to the alternatives so that it doesn't hurt our economy.

The thing that is hard for most of us to understand is why our government can't seem to use common sense in dealing with foreign policy. If we continue to become indebted to foreign powers and cater to their wishes, it won't be long before we are a super power in name only. The sad part is it could easily be corrected. Once again all we have to do is vote out the incumbents in public office until they decide to listen to what we have to say.

Chapter 8

Conclusion

If we're honest, we all have to admit that there are many problems in the good old U.S.A. All you have to do is pick up a paper or turn on the evening news and you will hear of all kinds of crimes being committed, how bad our economy is, illegal immigration issues and much more. While we may never be able to fix all the problems, we have to start somewhere.

One of the biggest obstacles in solving issues and making our country great again is apathy. We don't seem to care about the problems we have like we should. We gripe and complain about the way things are and talk about the good old days, but we never step up to do anything about the situation. After much consideration, I believe that people fall into one of three categories that explain their apathy.

The first category is the helpless or guilty category. I believe that the majority of Americans fall into this category. It is the one that best identifies how I feel. People in this category want to do something to make our country great again, but they feel like they can't because, after all, what can just one person do. They are also afraid if they speak out they will be rebuked because what they say may offend someone. The whole situation just seems so overwhelming to those of us in this group and so we do nothing.

What I find funny is this is probably the biggest group and if they would speak out, they would get things accomplished. I have a friend that falls into this group and for good reason. He once spoke out against some injustices that were occurring in his work place to some of the female workers. He told me that the majority of the workers in the office told him that they agreed with him and they were behind him one hundred percent. He should have known there was a problem when the people that told him this made sure no one else was around when they said it.

Because he took a stand, management had to make some changes and things improved. My friend had been with this company for about four years and all of his performance reviews had been excellent. Within three months of him standing up to management, his next review went very bad and the Georgia based company exercised their right to terminate him without reason. He decided to get a lawyer and sue for his job back, but quickly dropped this idea after he talked with some of his fellow employees. None of them were willing to testify for him because they were afraid they would lose their job. They agreed with him, but they didn't want to take a chance on being fired. The sad part is that if they had all stood together from the very beginning, the company would have had a hard time letting any of them go.

It's the same with those of us in this group. We want to do something, but we're afraid to try and we feel alone in our views. I believe that this group is the silent majority in this country.

The second category is the people who don't care because they don't see how it affects them. I believe this is probably a relatively small group, made up mostly of highly affluent people that have either profited from the way things are, or just haven't been affected yet by the problems we have. These people don't get concerned until the problems we have start to cause them to change their lifestyle.

I was talking to a potential client once who is the best example I can think of for this group. We were talking about upcoming elections and he asked me my views on the subject. I shared them with him even though I've been warned many times that you should never discuss religion or politics at work. My feeling is that we should all be discussing politics every chance we can because it's the only way to bring issues to the fore front of the public and possibly get something done. Anyway, after I shared my views, I asked him what he thought. This very wealthy man, who makes hundreds of tough choices every week, looked me in the eye and said he didn't really care because it didn't affect him, so he didn't even think he was going to vote. It took all I had not to lose my cool and berate the man. Instead, I took a few minutes to share some different things that might affect him in the future. I'm not sure it did any good, but at least I could say I tried.

The people in this group are more likely to get involved if something that the government does starts to affect them. That's what makes this group dangerous to me, because they are so apathetic until it affects them and then they start to throw their money around to try and get things done.

The third category is the fantasy world people. These people have a special kind of apathy. They tell themselves that it doesn't matter what our government does, eventually things will get better. They don't feel a need to try to do anything because they think things will eventually correct themselves.

I had an uncle that fit perfectly into this category. He was always optimistic and truly believed that things would get better eventually if we just sat back and gave it time. I would try to argue politics with him, but he would always say the same thing. "It doesn't matter who we elect, we're going to have good and bad times, but the country will always correct itself." Now, you have to remember, he came up through hard times and saw things get much better before he died. The problem is, even in the worst times he went through, our country was never in the debt that it is now. It was more self sufficient and less reliant on other countries. Rome went through a lot of good times before it finally collapsed.

Don't misunderstand me, I don't think we are so close to the brink of collapse that we can't turn things around, but we have to start the process. The way the world is set up today, I don't think the U.S. would totally collapse, but I do think we could become a very weak nation that has to bow to the wishes of the growing economic powers of the world like China.

The good news is that we still have time to turn things around and become a strong super power again. Unfortunately I don't think we can do it without a major overhaul of our political machine. The way things are set up now, nothing ever seems to get done. It's the same old ineffective solutions to the same old problems.

We want to blame our politicians, but in reality we have no one to blame but ourselves.

Fixing America

Our nation continues to go down because we refuse to act. My wife has been a teacher for over twenty years now. She enjoyed the first twelve to fourteen years of her teaching career, but for the last seven it has become harder for her to enjoy her job. The reason for this is the parents and children that she has to deal with now. Many of the parents seem to think that their children can do no wrong and they don't seem to support the teachers like prior generations did. Not all of the parents are like this, but we allow the ones that are to dominate our school system. My wife has complained many times that she spends the majority of her day trying to bring two or three students in line and up to the same level as the other students in her class.

    The problem is that parents don't want to take responsibility for correcting their kids or teaching them what they need to succeed in life. They want the government to take on the task of raising their kids and the government is all to willing to try, but as usual they are failing.

    I remember when I was about ten years of old, my dad caught me and three other boys getting ready to smoke a cigarette in his utility building that had several gas cans with gas fumes built up in them. My dad beat all of our butts and then told the other parents what happened and they all took their turns beating our butts. That was pretty much the end of my smoking days. I didn't like having my butt beat, but I knew that my dad did it because he loved me and didn't want me to do something that could cause me harm. The funny thing is that the other three guys thought the world of my dad and even came to his funeral years later to pay their respects. All three brought up that incident and talked about how it changed their lives.

    I bring this up as an example of how our society has gone down and how we have sat back and let it happen. When I was a kid most parents were like my dad. They spoke out when they saw injustices in our society. Now we are all into being so politically correct, that we're afraid to say anything when we see people do something wrong. Think about when you're standing in a long line patiently waiting your turn. You've been in the line for about forty minutes and probably have another thirty minute wait ahead of you. A man walks up and sees the line and then sees someone close to the front that he knows. He walks up and starts talking to the person and then slowly works his way in to the line right behind his friend. Everyone in the line wants to say something, but no one does. Nobody wants to make a scene, so everyone gripes and complains among themselves, but they don't speak out.

This may seem like an insignificant example, but you can apply it to many things in our society. Most of us feel disgusted and fed up with the way things are going in our society. We complain about all the problems we have, but we don't do anything about it. We continue to vote the same politicians into office and we continue to let political correctness influence our decisions rather than speaking out and doing the right thing.

My grandfather used to tell me that doing the right thing was hard most of the time, but you sure could sleep better at night. Whenever we are faced with any issue in life, we have to ask ourselves what is the right thing to do and then do it.

What's the right thing for us to do now in order to make our society great again? That's the tough question that we have to ask. When I asked myself this question, I came up with many answers and then I narrowed it to the six areas I've listed in this book that we need to begin with in order to fix America.

The next thing I did was ask myself how do I get these things implemented to start improving our society. I have to admit that when I thought about how hard it would be to get change accomplished in our current system, I almost felt like giving up and not writing this book. I had to keep telling myself that change starts with one person willing to stand up and speak out.

There was a man once that spoke out against the controlling government of his time. He was a farmer in Virginia who was tired of being overly taxed and mistreated by the government. He and several others spoke out, even though it was unpopular to do so. Most people agreed with them, but their stance was unpopular because people were afraid of the consequences if they spoke out.

This man led a small band of under fed and under clothed men against a much superior force and won. You've probably figured out by now that the man I'm talking about was George Washington. Today we see him as one of the founders of our country, but we don't really think about what he truly risked to achieve all that he did. If England had won the war, Washington and all of the other leaders of the Revolutionary War would have been tried and executed for treason. By doing this, they insured the freedom of speech that we have today.

The problem is that we have had to risk very little in our life time and we now take a lot of our freedoms for granted. We've all settled into our little comfort zone and as long as that is not affected in a big way, we just go along with the status quo. Our government knows this and so they chip away at our comfort zone just a little at a time, because we're not as likely to put up a fight if they do it that way.

Our current situation with gas prices is a perfect example. Oil companies have continually raised the price for gas over the last two years. Our government wants to blame it on foreign oil production. They don't tell you that most of the problem is due to their lack of creating enough refineries or doing off shore drilling. What they do instead is allow the prices to climb until people start to cut back on usage, then they will get the oil companies to drop the prices back by twenty five to thirty cent per gallon. They will leave it there until consumption goes back up and people adjust to the price. Then they will slowly increase the prices again until the thirty cent reduction is wiped out and it continues to increase until we start to consume less again. They know that if they can get us used to something over a long enough period of time, then we will put up with about anything.

If we continue in this pattern, then we will slowly lose many of the freedoms that we have. We can't continue to blame politicians for our failure to act. We have to take a long look at ourselves. When we allow certain behaviors to occur over and over, we tend to start considering the behaviors as just another part of life and we begin to feel like there is nothing we can do. Besides, it's not really affecting us so we can just kind of look the other way. Eventually, however, we do have to pay a price for our lack of action.

When I was a kid, I remember that most of the movies that came out were G-rated. There were a few R-rated ones but not very many. When I was fifteen a friend's Dad took me to see Mad Max with Mel Gibson. It was the first R-rated movie that I had ever seen and I remember feeling almost sick to my stomach from the violence that I saw. Since that time I've seen many R-rated movies with lots of violence. Recently I saw Mad Max on television and it was almost laughable. It made me realize how desensitized I have become to the things that I watch. It occurred over a long period of time and took me the same amount of time to figure out what had happened. I don't really know how violence in movies has affected society; I just know how it affected me. It hasn't made me more violent, but it has allowed me to be indifferent to the violence I see.

The same thing seems to be happening to a lot of us as far as what we are willing to over look in our political system. Look at the number of politicians that have been involved in sex scandals and still remain in office. Even worse to me is the number of politicians who have been involved in shady financial dealings and yet we continue to vote them in.

It's time that we change the way things are done. The first step is to stop listening to just the news media and forming our opinion based on their reports. We need to check politicians out for ourselves and do a little homework before we decide who we are going to vote for.

Next we need to stop letting celebrity's influence which candidate we choose. Just because someone is famous doesn't mean they know what they are talking about. Truth be told, most of these celebrities don't do their homework any better than we do.

Next we need to leave race and sex out of our decision. We need to do our research on each of the candidates and base our decision on who we feel will do the best job. It shouldn't matter if they're black, white, Hispanic, male or female. It should be based purely on their record and if we feel they are the best person for the job.

Finally, we need to act when our politicians fail to do so. When they refuse to do the will of the people, then we need to use the power of our vote to remove them from office. We should be shaking up Congress every election period until these politicians understand that they are there to represent us and failure to do so will cost them their job.

Most of the people in positions of power would say that it's just not that simple, but I have to disagree. The answer to our problems are simple, it just takes hard work and hard decisions to get it done. Like I said before, the last two generations have had very little adversity to face and it has caused us to become complacent.

As I said in the beginning, I'm just a common man with enough common sense to know that the current system is not working. It's time to try something different and use common sense to fix our nation. If we continue the way we are going, things definitely won't get better. If we continue to do the same old thing, we're going to continue to get the same old results. In this book I've outlined six areas to begin with; the only thing left to do is to force the politicians to start working on implementing the solutions. From here on out, it's up to us. Will we step up and make the changes we need to, or will we continue in the same destructive ways? It's time to choose.

About the Author

Tim Smith was born in Kannapolis, North Carolina, a small textile mill community. At the age of eight, Tim started mowing yards and has since worked in both blue and white collar positions. Tim is now an independent insurance agent and author. He is married, has four children, and currently resides in Gwinnett County, GA. Tim is currently working on his second book in which he tells the story of how he was brutally attacked and how his faith in God has helped him deal with the life-altering injuries.

www.ingramcontent.com/pod-product-compliance
Lightning Source LLC
Chambersburg PA
CBHW021859170526
45157CB00005B/1889